Nothing to laugh about

by len munnik

A Fellowship Book

The Pilgrim Press
New York

Library of Congress Cataloging in Publication Data

Munnik, Len, 1945-
    Nothing to laugh about.

    1. Atomic weapons—Caricatures and cartoons.
2. Dutch wit and humor, Pictorial.   I. Title.
U264.M8513   1983   355.8'25119'0207   83-13173
ISBN 0-8298-0694-6 (pbk.)

The Pilgrim Press, 132 West 31 Street, New York, N.Y. 10001

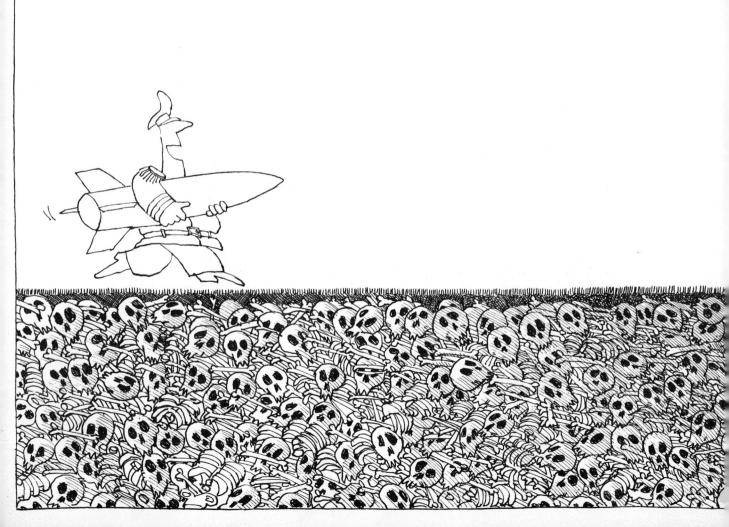

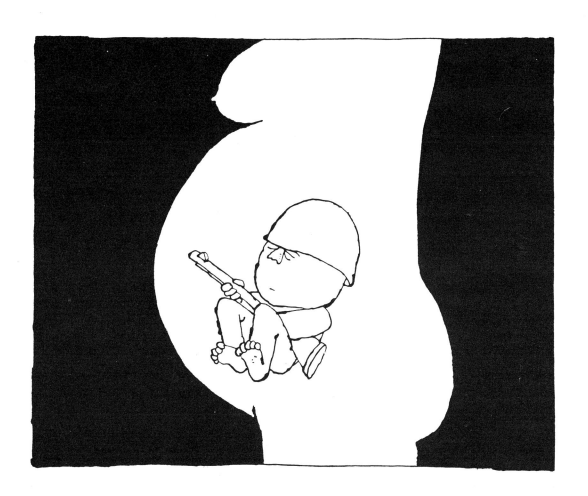

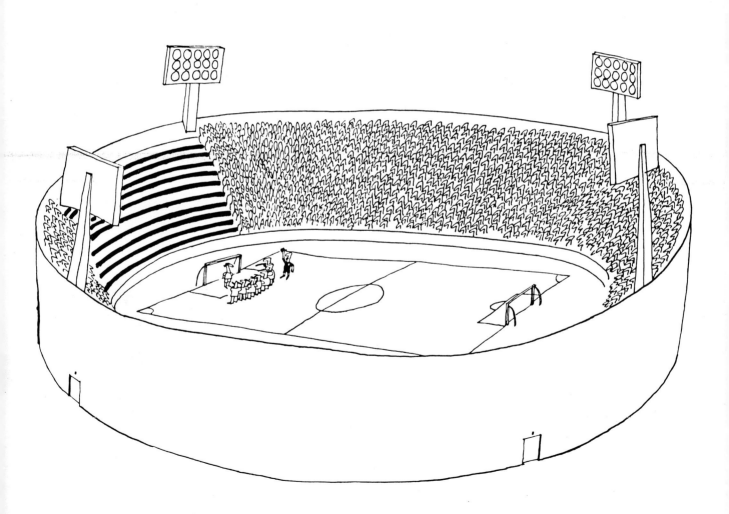

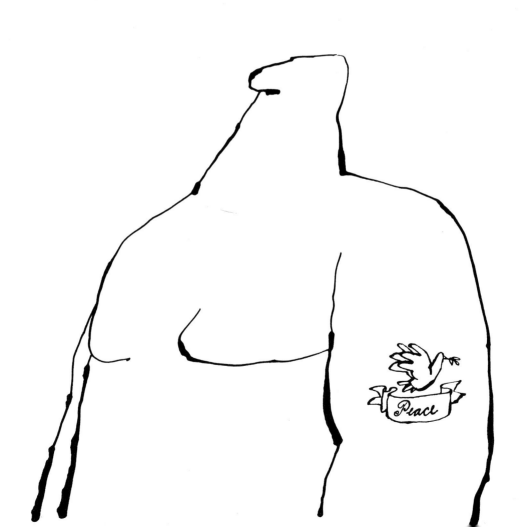

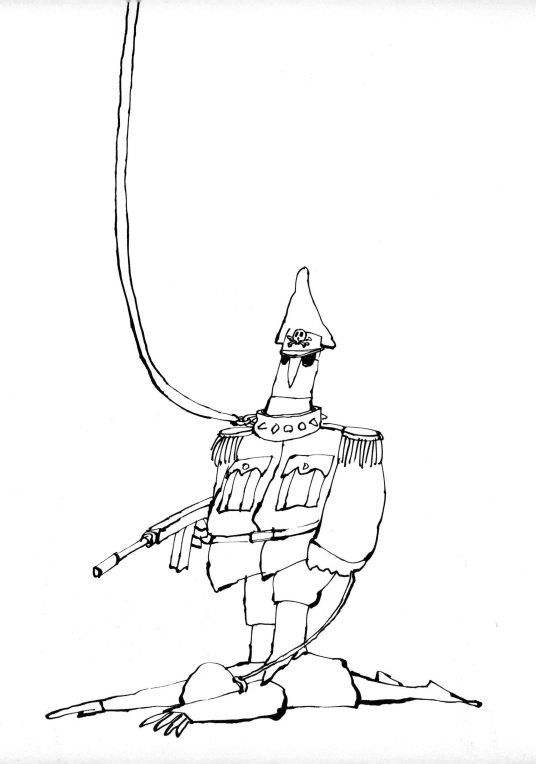

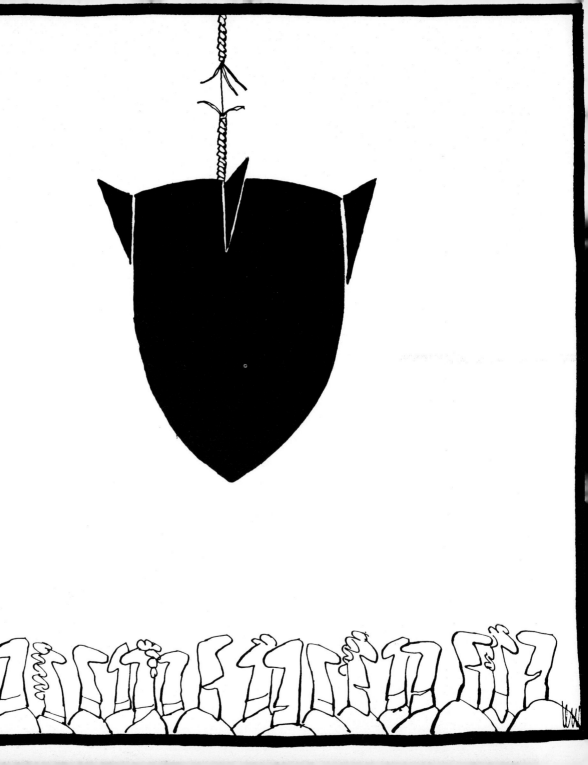

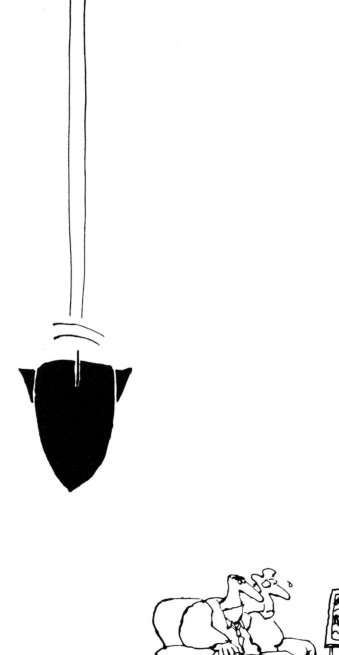

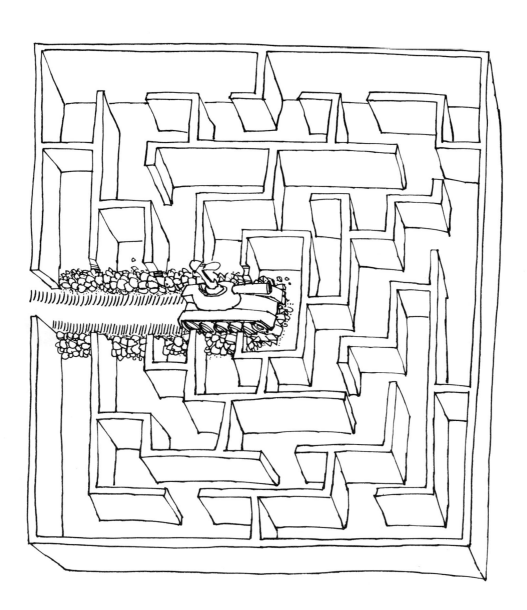

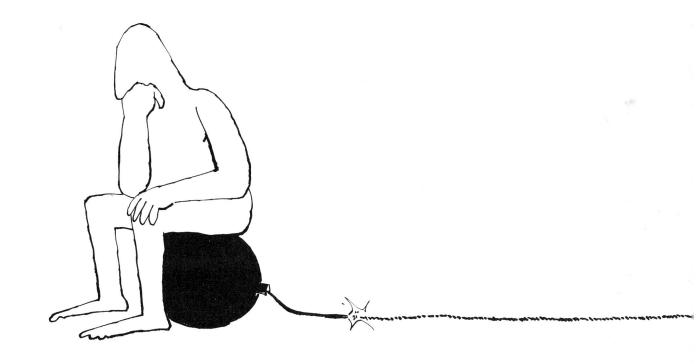

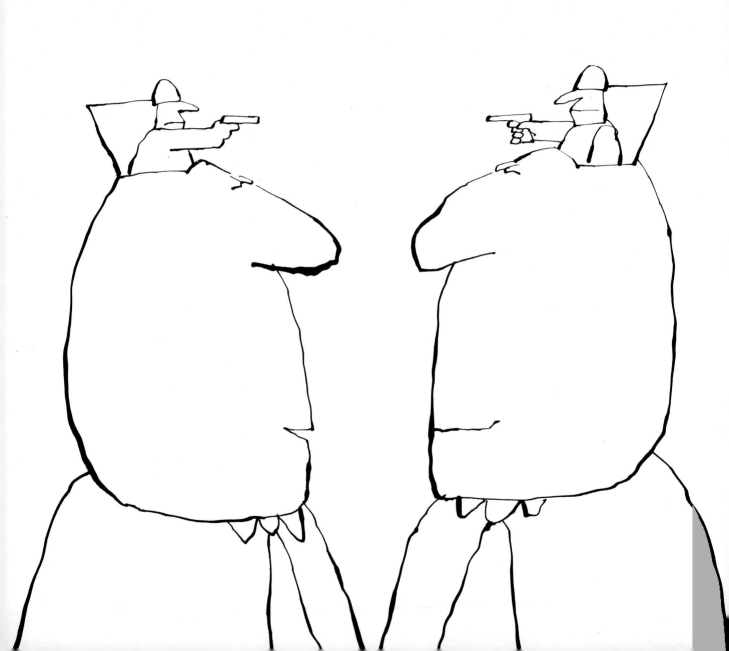

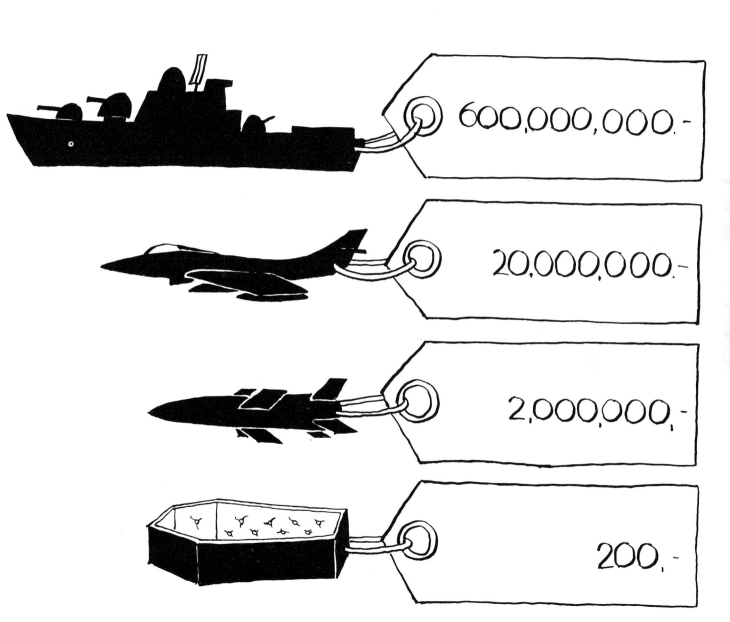

REAGAN

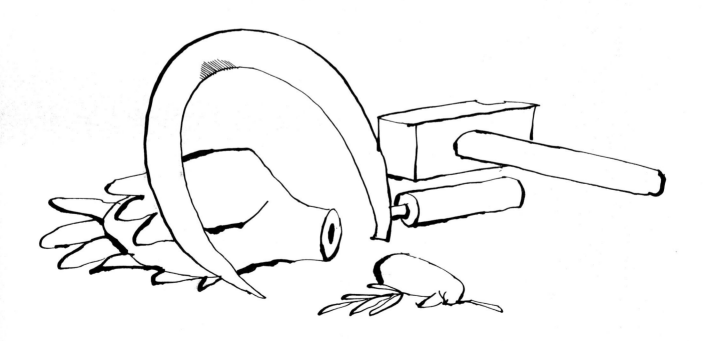

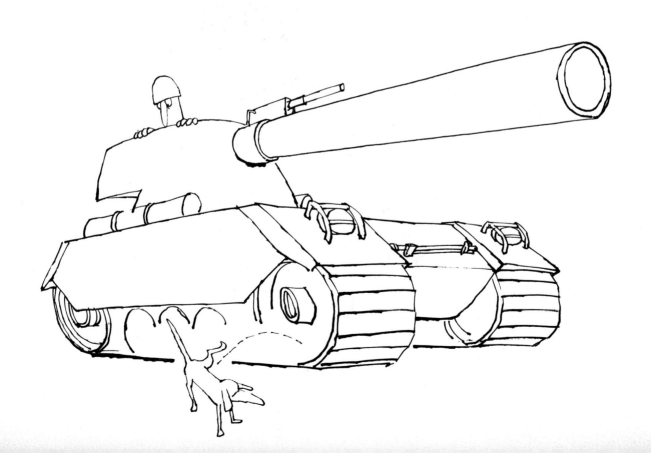

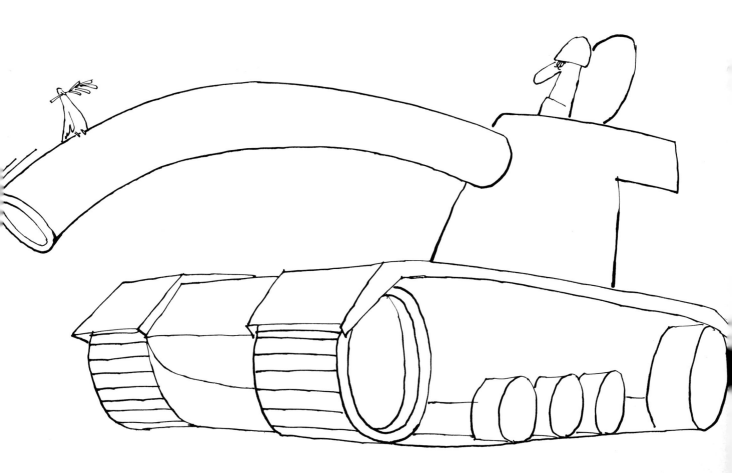

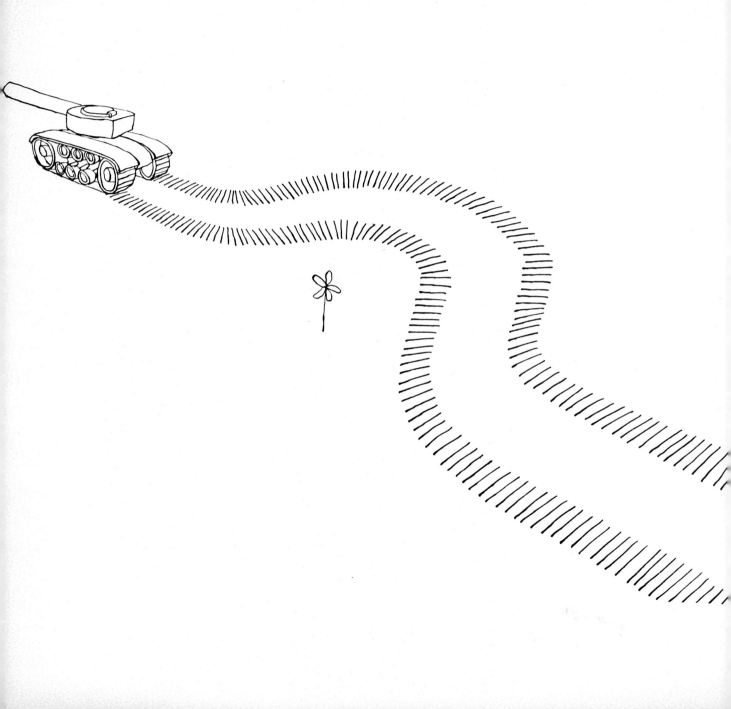

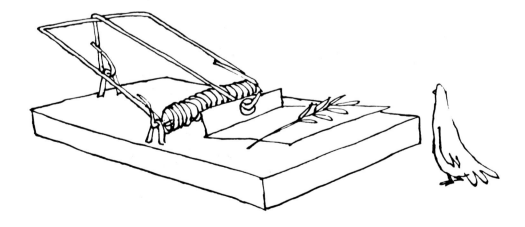

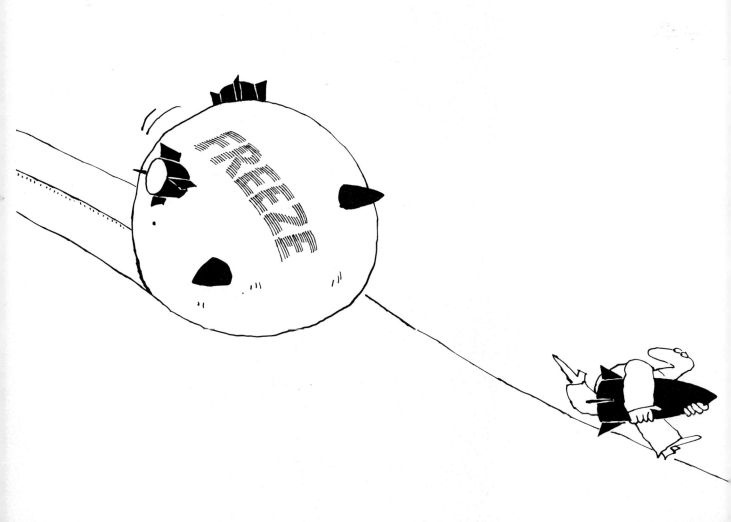